Silent

Cries of a

BLEEDING

HEART

Table of Contents

Letter to readers

A word to the wise.

To: My readers

From: Dasheen P. White

I was born March 20, 1973 in Queens, NY by way of James White and Pauline Austin. I have been once widowed and twice divorced. I am the proud mother of Taurence Scott II, Tiphanie Smith and Christian Thomas. I have seven beautiful grandchildren; Grace Scott, Gaia & Luna Smith and Phoenix Thomas, Sean and Amya.

It is my pleasure to share my journey of healing and freedom with you. My desire is that you will learn, be blessed and grow from each poem that you read in this book. Most importantly understand that you are not alone in your struggles. There is always someone going through the same thing that you are facing or worse but through it all we can help one another overcome. We don't have to be stuck in our circumstances.

I wrote this book because like many of you I have been through my share of ups and downs. I have experienced a lot of heartache and disappointments and most times I don't feel very successful in dealing with them. When I write I get a sense of release. It is my vehicle to reach people who may be experiencing or have experienced the same challenges.

This book is a source of healing for me. I had to write it to get rid of all the pain, hatred, bitterness, and anger, the feelings of betrayal, abandonment and confusion. When I am done the door to every one of these emotional prisons will be closed. The yokes of bondage are being broken and the gate keepers are being displaced.

My son prophesied to me years ago that my poetry would be the vehicle of my deliverance. I received that word that day with all my heart. I just didn't know when it would be fulfilled. It is true that God's timing is not our timing, His ways are not our ways and His thoughts are higher than our thoughts.

I am grateful that my son has always been wise beyond his years and was obedient to share that bit of wisdom with me when God spoke into his heart

This day I declare my freedom in God. I am taking my power back from everyone that I have given it to. I have the power over how I allow someone, or something affect me.

Read at your own risk but leave your judgment behind. I must be transparent and completely honest with myself and bare it all to the world. Filtering my feelings to spare yours will not allow me to receive the healing I desire and need. It is imperative that I tell it like it is; leaving NOTHING uncovered. The longer I conceal my thoughts, ignore my battles and lie about the demons I wrestle with each day; the longer my sentence in this emotional prison; this place of bondage, this personal hell that I face each day. Step out of the box, take off the robe and throw down the gavel if you choose to read further. This journey is not for the closed-minded judgmental people.

Bleeding Heart

Pain, hurt, heaviness, confusion, despair

Looking for relief, peace and a way out

Longing for love, comfort and loyalty

My life seems so chaotic and hopeless

Running fast but getting nowhere

Climbing but always falling back down

I realize that all I am doing; all I have done

None of it is producing the results or the goals I am trying to reach

So I stop to refocus

I must regroup

There is a lesson to be learned

A moral to be taught

The rat race is over

One day at a time

One hour, each minute counts

I'll deal with one issue in each moment

I am not quite where I want to be, but am on my
way

Reaching for my destiny

Learning my purpose

And fulfilling my dreams

(Untitled)

I have been waiting for this moment all week; this moment to empty my cup but something very strange takes place when I grab my pencil and attempt to put it to paper.

I draw a blank; unable to express the many thoughts that have been invading my mind space all week.

There is so much to say; so many questions I need answered.

How do I relay my message, pose my question and express my feelings?

A release is much needed. Who do I go to?

Who will be able to receive all that I have inside?

I find myself searching for emotional healing; looking for a way to acknowledge, understand and accept all that troubles me, not so I can stay where I am but to be able to receive the breakthrough and healing that is much needed.

This will be the only way I can move forward.

Many times, people have told me to give it to God, but they have never told me how.

How do I give something that I have protected & carried with me all my life to someone I have not allowed myself to fully trust?

I want to let go. I want to trust Him the way I should, but I don't know how to be vulnerable to anyone else.

I have spent so much of my life trying to protect myself from being taken advantage of by anyone else that I just don't know how to let go.

Fearing that when I finally open up to someone, they will discover that am so messed up they will turn and run as fast as they can; never looking back.

So I come to you Lord seeking your guidance of how to accept myself for who I am.

I need your help to recognize my issues, acknowledge them and give them over to you for complete release and deliverance.

No longer do I want to look at myself and experience instant disappointment blaming myself for the many failures, betrayals and abandonment I have experienced in my life.

I believe when I can do that I can move forward.

When I can stop going back through the old chapters of my life; looking behind me at what used to be…then and only then will I be able to move forward.

Noise Pollution

Thoughts of my present

Regrets of my past

Anxieties of my future

So much is running through my head

I can't seem to turn it off

The noise of confusion, regret and disappointment

Trying to find a quiet place

It's impossible because everywhere I go my
thoughts go with me

Maybe if I say it out loud get it off my chest

Temporary pleasures; a little peace

But this still doesn't bring the release I need

 I seek restitution, restoration and resolution

I need my issues to be resolved

Wisdom, guidance and direction to point me down
the right path

Lead me down the path that will break the vicious
cycles I have kept alive

Put an end to the insanity of doing things the same over and over expecting different results

Quite the thoughts that are killing me faster than cancer

Minister to me in your infinite wisdom that will teach me lessons from my past

Give me discernment when dealing with my present, faith to trust you with my future and strength to let go of my past

Life's Lessons

The most brutal teacher I have ever encountered is life.

She will teach you things no man can ever phantom; no self-help book can ever provide, and no tutorial can ever break down.

The lessons life will educate you on must be experienced firsthand.

Each student must be attentive, willing to learn, positioned to receive and wise enough to obtain.

Life's messages will either tear you down or build you up.

They will either rip you apart or put you back together again.

Through your journey you must keep your eyes open & your mind fresh.

Never think that you know it all, ask plenty of questions and always seek after wisdom.

Don't be a clone, dare to be different and be courageous enough to release anything and anyone that weighs you down.

Grab hold to all that will catapult you to the next level.

Life is the hardest teacher you will ever encounter but the most affective.

It is up to you what you take from her or throw away.

Foolish Eyes

What I saw and who you really are; are a contradiction, a foolish premonition.

A dream I wanted to be true.

I thought I found an answer to my prayers, but I discovered it was mirage.

You knew all the right things to do; when, where and how.

The connection was unreal; too good to be true...Literally!

When the dust cleared the blow to my heart was deadly.

I refused to believe that an illusion could feel so real.

I refused to let go.

My heart clung to the memories so tight I was suffocating myself with the smoke from the fire that burned in my heart for you.

Each breath I took hurt so deeply because the weight that lay so heavily on my chest.

I knew that I must release you, but my foolish eyes kept replaying the visions of the one-sided love that I thought we both shared.

It was like trying to shake myself to wake up from a bad dream.

You know the one when you think you are screaming loudly but it is really under your breath and it is never loud enough for anyone else to hear. Yeah, that's the one.

But just as it is with that bad dream once you finally are able to open your eyes and see that none of it was real; reality sets in. only I don't feel relief right away because I have to regroup and begin to face the truth.

It was only a fantasy; a dream of deception that my foolish eyes put together for me.

The Noose

You walked into my life hypnotizing me with your smooth words of dreams goals and aspirations

You mesmerized me with the love I thought you had for me

With each lie, each promise the noose got tighter and tighter until I was at your mercy, under your control

You left me hanging, gasping for air

Fighting for my life struggling

Trying to find a way break free

I feel myself fading in and out of consciousness

You come back and loosen the rope a little every now and then

Promising me that one day you'll set me free and then you leave

I must find a way to cut this rope and get this noose from around my neck; never putting it back on again

I must get my heart out of your clutches before you cause any further damage

Life's Classroom

Let your mistakes teach you not torcher you

Remember but do not agonize over the things you have experienced

There will be plenty of disappointments in life

But do not let any of them haunt you

Do not reminisce on each event

Let them be teachable moments

A lesson that you will never repeat

As you strive for perfection; remember that you are human

You are fallible

Let it make you better not bitter

Do not hold hatred, anger or unforgiveness in your heart

Do not seek revenge on those that wronged you

They too held an important key to your life lesson

They were vessels carrying bitter messages you had to gain information from

However, you must release them for the healing you
need

Take back your power

Forgive them and set yourself free

Abused Love

Like a stake to the heart

A punch to the gut; love will take your breath away

It will make your heart bleed

Like the most potent drug on the street; it will distort your thinking and blur your vision

Love will squeeze you and render you lifeless; paralyzing you leaving you delirious and confused

It will have you walking cautiously through life

At times feeling like you are walking through a minefield

If not handled properly; love will run through your veins like a deadly venom

Slowly sucking the life out of you

Killing anything in you of value

Love will hypnotize you like watching a car accident

You want to look away, but you are drawn to the mangled heap of metal

Captured by the tangled mess

In the wrong hands, love is dangerous and very deadly

It's like putting a scalpel in the hands of a small child

Expecting them to perform surgery

In the end you are left with a nasty bloody mess, an unnecessary death

Love is not to be misused or abused

(Untitled)

We don't work because we are at two different ends
of the spectrum

You want my body and I want your heart

You don't want a relationship until you finish going
through your issues

I want to grow through our issues together

You are satisfied having the illusion of what a real
relationship looks like

I want to create the relationship that erases the
illusion that it can't exist

You say you love me and for a moment my heart
skipped a beat but then reality snatched me by the
neck and calmed me down really quick

There is always so much conflict when I think of us

The way I feel vs what you want, what I want vs
what you need, what you say vs what I see

It is all so confusing; I can't recognize the truth

Silent Cries

I am screaming and no one hears me

I am wounded and no one is near to stop the bleeding

I feel as if I am near death

I am screaming, screaming into the night

Somebody; Please, help me

I am growing weaker, my vision is getting dim

I'm here in the darkest corner of the room

The place where no one dares to go

Please, don't leave me here

I know I have made mistakes and let some of you down unawares

But you said you love me and yet I feel so alone

Is anyone willing to help me through?

There is a silent killer desiring my life

Working diligently to take me out

Squeezing, squeezing ever so tightly

I am doing all I know to survive

I am fighting for my life

But it's pulling, pulling on my soul

I'm fighting and holding on with everything in me

It feels like I have reached the end of my fight

Like I have nothing left

Fading, fading ever so quickly

Will anyone reach me before I fade away?

I am here, over here in the darkest part of the room where no one dares to go

Silent cries, countless tears

Does anyone hear?

Can anyone see?

These silent cries; so soft so weak

Roller Coaster

(Love)

The motion of this roller coaster is making me sick

I want to cry so badly but I can't breathe

So, I choke back the tears

Praying for it to be over

I know I must endure the ride until it's done

I shut my eyes as tight as I can

Tensing every muscle in my body

Feeling the up and down motion; daring not to open my eyes

I feel myself rising to the peak of the tracks

I don't want to see the drop that follows

The only thing that keeps me sane is knowing that it will eventually be over

Vowing never to take this ride again

Finally, I dismount the seat that held me in

Legs wobbly like a toddler taking their first steps

Looking back, I realize the arms of the Lord were tightly wrapped around me, holding me, securing me there.

Letting nothing knock me off course

It was Him that got me to the end

Surprisingly I take I find myself back in line to take the ride again

Crossroads

I am standing here at a crossroad

Looking at so many signs

It's all so confusing

Each sign has its own direction and warnings

Signs telling me to exit here, get on there

Stay straight, bare to the left

Swing right, take a sharp turn here

Avoid the underpass

Which way do I go? I really don't know

So, I stand still daring not to move

Knowing that one wrong turn can take me on a trip
to nowhere and a long journey back to where I
began

I stand here waiting patiently, looking at each sign,
waiting for one of them to be clear

Determined to take the right road

Waiting patiently; standing at this road of decisions
trying not to panic

Patiently I wait

My Destiny

I flow because I have not allowed this world to destroy my destiny

I speak life that moves obstacles that try to create blockage in my spiritual veins

I boldly command those things that destroy hope and bring death to cease its existence

My words carry the power to tear down the walls that make it impossible to reach the other side

I will reach success

Failure is not an option

I am the wrecking ball that make negative structures crumble

I come with force, focus and determination

Power is in my possession and it trumps any weakness that would try to take me out

I will not believe that I cannot do anything

Fear must bow to me

It has no strength or influence over my dreams or aspirations

I don't acknowledge failures as a force that can stop me, but only brief pauses in my life that allow me to step back and regroup

I see them as opportunities to go over the notes of my life

Putting things into perspective; recognizing failures and successes

Keeping those things that enhanced my growth and throwing away those things that extracted value from my being

I control my destiny

I am

I am the wrecking ball that knocks down the walls of Satan

I am the truth that makes lies tremble

I am the power that makes weakness bow down and acknowledge authority

I am the root that gave birth to a way of growth; she who is Christ like and the appearance of God

I am the grandmother of unmerited favor and the spiritual mother of a princess

I am the daughter of the King and the heir of the Prince of Peace

I am who God says I am, not the thoughts of society or a statistic

I am not a failure

I walk in success and not defeat

I stand out and not blend in

This worlds system is not the path I follow

I follow blueprints of the master builder

This world is not my home

I am a resident of the kingdom that cannot be duplicated

I am royalty

Hush

Shhh; too much noise

Too many memories

A multitude of questions

Unfinished puzzles

Crowded thoughts

Shh, shh, shh

Quiet. I need silence

I can't think

So much confusion

Noting makes sense

I need peace

I need relief

When will the racket end?

When will the noise stop?

When will I be free of these thoughts that haunt me?

These thoughts that cause so much pain

Shhh; peace come now

Wait no longer

Shhh, Shhh, Shhh

Through the Storm

Rough waters

Blistering winds

Dark clouds

Blinding rain

The storm is strong and difficult to get through

But I must keep pushing

Pushing through the elements

Determined to get to the other side

I must not stop; I refuse to give up

Battered and bruised

Cold and wet; a little weary from fighting against
the wind

Somewhat relieved; I see a break in the storm

Clouds begin to separate

The rain has ceased

Rays of sunshine begin to peak through

A breath of fresh air

A sigh of relief

The storm is over

I made it through

A new day begins

Behind the Smile

Smiles are easily misread

Most times we smile to keep from crying

We smile to hide the pain

Deep down inside we are riddled with confusion

Overwhelmed with trials

Full of hidden tears

Crushed by countless betrayals

Left empty due to abandonment

Starving because of desires

Longing for answers and fulfillment

Frustrated because of unspent gifts lying dormant inside of us

Suspicious because of doubt and distrust

Disappointed because of failures

Housing feelings of inadequacies because of physical and or mental abuse

Wanting so badly to turn things around

Exhausted from the constant battle on the inside

Doing all that you can not to walk in fear

But desperately holding on to the ounce of faith that has not faded with the smile that you wear to mask the multitude of emotions that are trying to erase who you are.

There is so much hidden behind a smile.

Invisible

I am surrounded by deaf and blind people

They have ears but they hear nothing

They have eyes but they do not see

I do not speak of the physically impaired

I speak of those who are so consumed with themselves that hurting people go unnoticed

The needy are not recognized and the hungry get ignored

Our world has lost sight of what is important

It is a lonely place to be when you have no voice and you feel invisible

It is like dyeing a slow death with no one around to hear your weak desperate cries

Struggling, praying and hoping that someone will hear you or glance your way long enough to realize you desperately need help

Anticipation and desperation set in

Frustration and anger take over

This world cannot be so selfish that no one sees the need for help or hears the desperate cries or feels the urge to step up and rescue me

People can't you see.

Toxic Relationship

The venom you released from your lips poisoned my heart, bringing a slow death to the love I once longed for

Your words were infectious; full of deception, covered up with lies that clouded and compromised my thinking

They provided a temporary filler an unhealthy satisfaction for the love I longed for

Even with the truth that has been revealed to me; there is such a division in my heart

The battle of what I know, what I wanted and what has to be

It still baffles my mind that someone can masquerade a love so well; convince one that it really exists and then shut it down as if it were never there

I guess I should have been relieved when you chose to discontinue your act; however, I am not immune to pain

I only hope that one day; the man you pretended to be will one day be the one you become

Release

Terrified; trying to move forward

Constantly remembering my past

Wanting so desperately to move forward

But hoping somehow that this bad dream will end

Doing everything I can to start over again

Trying not to die in my emotions or lose myself in
what was

This is scary.

My memories haunt me, my anger taunts me and
my heart refuses to let go

How do I begin again?

Will all of this confusion ever end?

No one ever told me that starting over could be such
a lonely crazy place

None-the-less; I am moving forward

I must shake myself, face reality and weather the
storm

Accept that this isn't a dream, face my fears and
push past my emotions

I will waist no more time on what could have been
and invest in my future

I am starting over again

You Can Make It

It's over now and that's okay

You will survive this if you stay focused

This is your moment

The time in your life where you can live

Explore and learn who you are

Discover what you like

You have spent your entire life learning others; trying to figure out what would make others happy

Reach down inside of you and get your power back

Regain all that you lost in each relationship

Let every stumbling block be a steppingstone

Leave your past alone

You are strong, vibrant and successful

You can make it

Let go of all the disappointments

It's time for you to make your dreams come true

Keep a positive mind

Strive for success

This is your time

Your moment in life

 If you keep your head up

Never give up

You can make it.

Friend

A true friend walks in when the rest of the world walks out

When it feels like you have lost everything and there is no hope

A smile, a warm embrace is all you need.

They never really have to say a word; there presence is enough

A friend is someone you can count on

When you're weak and at your all time low in their presence you don't feel judged but understood and accepted

They can correct you when you're wrong and when you're right they cheer you on

They will laugh with you in times of happiness and cry with you when you're down

A friend will loath your defeats and celebrate your victories

They will be with you in the beginning and strive with you until the end

This to me is a true friend

(Untitled)

I find myself constantly searching for my next move

Right now, nothing seems very clear

I see God moving in my life, but I know there is much work to be done

I acknowledge that I need to surrender so much more of myself to Him

My mind feels like a traffic jam

There are so many thoughts running through my head

 So much that I want

Things I want to see

Which way do I go?

What shall I do?

It is dangerous to move to slow

I certainly can't stand still

I cannot be too hasty

It is vital that I make the right decisions

There isn't much room for mistakes

I would be naïve to think I won't slip up sometimes,
but I must act wisely; move timely and plan
strategically

Giving up is not an option

Failure will not be accepted

Quitting is not in my blood

I will reach my destiny

(Untitled)

Why can't I get you out of my mind?

I don't understand why it is so difficult to close this door

Why must my heart long after you so

I feel like a fool chasing dreams and shadows

You have made it clear that I am not who you want to be with and here is not where e you want to be

When will this pain end?

When will the longing go away?

When will you no longer be a thought that haunts my mind?

When will the pain stop tearing my heart apart?

I want to hate you so bad, but I can't stop loving you

Why must I continue to suffer?

Will I ever be free of this burden; this weight that continues to crush my heart

I never thought that love would feel like a parasite eating me up on the inside

I certainly never thought you would be the one to break my heart leaving me here with shattered pieces

(Untitled)

I hear you loud and clear, but my heart chooses to
ignore the words that are coming out of your mouth

Why won't let go? Can my will to love you be this
stubborn or am I just afraid that if you won't love
me that no one will?

I look into your eyes and hope to see the love you
once had for me but it is no longer there

Am I so desperate for love that I will accept the pity
you give me; knowing that you don't feel of share
the same desires as I do?

You give me many reasons for your need to be
away from and none of them make sense. None of
them seem real or genuine

Your reasons and explanations do not give me the
closure I need to end this chapter.

I guess that is why it is so difficult to move forward;
there was no end to our beginning and the middle
had no real definition

I go back repeatedly and read each chapter very
carefully and each time it leaves me more confused

So, today, I choose a new quest

A quest to let go of the past and a goal to move toward my future

No bitterness, envy, hatred or confusion

Letting go of the need to know why and understanding that not everything can be in my control

Today, I let go!

Almost There

I'm so close I can feel it

The sweet taste of victory

It's right at the tip of my tongue

Carefully watching every sign

Strategically planning each step along the way

Doing everything I can not to repeat history

Praying not to be blinded by any familiar series of events

Positioning myself for this new place I am soon to enter

I pray for the state of mind that will prevent me from missing any blessings God has for me and the ability to grab hold to my dreams while they are in my reach

That Kind of Love

I want that heart racing, stomach jumping anxious
feeling, I can't wait 'til he gets off work kind of
love

That rapid breathing because he just touched me kin
d of love

I want that weak in the knees after he kisses me
kind of love

You know that kind of love that causes your friends
to ask where you are because your eyes glazed over
when you mentally left the room; Yeah, that kind of
love

The kind of love that makes you leave reality
because your mind is still basking in last night;
physically you are present but flashbacks took you
on a trip to cloud nine; Uh huh…That kind of love

I want that kind of love that causes you to smile
when you think of him

The kind of love that causes a smile to slloowwlly
part your lips when you think of the cute little
things, he does

Yeah, yeah; that kind of love

You feel me; right?

Yeeaahh; you know what I'm talking about

I want that kind of love

(Untitled)

Love does not tear down; it builds up

It does not criticize; it corrects

Love does not bring sorrow; it brings joy

Love does not manipulate; it congratulates

Love does not seek to hurt; it brings healing

Love does not bring chaos; it comforts

Love does not abuse it values

Don't cheat yourself by settling

Do not be bitter because they did not meet your expectations

They may be giving you the best of themselves

Just remember the choice to be together was a joint decision

Love is not solely dependence on in individual

It is the ability to independently love one another just for who you are and not losing your individuality

Love is not selfish but selfless

It does not block your blessings but pave a clear path for you to reach your destiny

Love does not masquerade but unveils

It does not confuse but bring clarity

It will not cripple you but give you the ability to move forward

Love is not paralyzing but gives mobility

Many times, people hold on to what they believe is love and in turn destroy who they are with bitterness and resentment because they do not understand why love is not being returned

It is not that love does not exist; it just is not present in the current relationship

(Untitled)

It pains me to say that I am here again. On the verge
of falling in love but you only want to be my friend

I want so bad to let go, to freely love you but my
heart is not built to endure what you will put it
through

Frustration overwhelms me as I replay the words
that entered my ears; the dirty truth that confirmed
my fears

Once again, I must reconstruct the wall of
protection that guarded my heart from unexpected
rejection

Denying myself the lust that masquerades as love
filling my heart with bitter infection

Guarding my heart from feelings of betrayal that are
birthed from deception

Is it my desires to be loved that attracts the same
type of men over and over again?

When will this cycle of destruction end?

Will I ever find my true love, or does that even exist
anymore?

With no regrets I am moving forward

No turning back; full steam ahead

I will not stop until my past thoughts no longer
haunt me

I will not punish myself for choosing freedom

Nor will I condemn myself for believing that I
deserve better

My heart is precious, and my love is valuable

I will not give either of them to anyone else who
does not want, appreciate or recognize their worth

Moving forward does not always feel good and it's
not always easy but it is definitely worth it

(Untitled)

I can remember sitting in a room full of people
dying, bleeding profusely from the wounds that life
inflicted upon me

Screaming silently and fighting through the pain

Desperately loping, praying that someone would
actually discern my suffering

Waiting for someone to rescue me but unfortunately
no one ever came

Numerous people just walked by stepping in pools
of my blood as I quickly faded away

Shaking their head in judgment because after all she
must not be doing something right

In all reality I have done all I know to do

I have sought counsel, prayed and trusted God for
all I need and I am still wondering if my process or
methods are wrong because here I lay on life
support fighting for what I was told I could have

Telling myself that I will live and not die

I have falling deeply but I will rise

It is my faith in the strength I once believed in; the
determination of wanting to win

The dream of one day looking back and saying wow
I have really grown

The stubbornness of knowing that one day I will get
through this even if I have to do it alone

(Untitled)

Not certain how things will work out but confident
that everything that led me here was divine planning

I am confident because I have peace, I have never
experienced in the midst of what appears to be
adverse transition.

Tears, heartache and confusion would normally be
the emotions consuming me

I feel peace and a drive to push, fight and reach the
top at any cost

A refusal to fail, give up or bow down to what I see
and a determination to reach what I want

My circumstances do not define me

I will bring definition to my life as my story unfolds

Keeping it 100

So many lay claims to this phrase

What does it mean anyway?

We get frustrated when one claims to keep it 100 and we find there were other motives underlining their actions

Truthfully, we cannot get mad at someone for coming short of our expectations

Take it for what it is and thank them for the revelation

To you they were perpetrating or being full of shit

But according to who they were being legit

A liar will never tell the truth

A cheater will never be faithful

A snake will forever slither around in the grass and if you get too close it will bite your ass

A weasel will faithfully sneak around doing mischievous deeds

And a gold digger will continue to be led by greed

Keeping it 100 will always be acted out by the nature of the individual and their inner drive

Just keep watch and be mindful of their actions and believe your eyes; they won't lie

They're just keeping it 100!

Renewed

Today I take my power back

Tomorrow I regain my strength

I will not weaken my spirit by magnifying all that I
gave away

When I remember things that were done to me

I will begin to give thanks

I will celebrate my survival; my ability to move on

I will rejoice in the fact that I am still standing

I will express gratefulness because I am able to
apply the lessons I learned and the wisdom that has
been imparted in me

The answers that I search for are not out there they
are within me

The choices I make determine my happiness and the
end to my sufferings

I choose my destiny

I will acknowledge the fact that the answers I seek
are in me

I will exercise the power I possess; identify the
problem and utilize the gifts entrusted to me

My past did not break me but empowered me for greatness

Strength

Strength is greatly underestimated, and many times misread

The world tells our boys if they cry, they are weak

Society has trained our little girls to believe if they can dominate and manipulate their man, they are strong

Each of these mentalities are false

Strongmen cry and powerful women know how to submit

Strength recognizes when to fight and when to let go

It knows what builds up and what tears down

Strength is knowing your worth and not letting anyone devalue you

Strength is trusting your heart only to those that will value it

Strength is standing tall when the world tries to break you down

It is loving yourself even when the one that should does not

It is relinquishing the need to be right

It is knowing when to take control or when to let go

Strength is the ability to use wisdom and
discernment in any situation

I Release you

I tried to hold on to the last string of faith

No promises made

No hope given

Time after time I have looked into your eyes,
listened to your words and witnessed your actions

Praying that something would spark that love you
once had for me

Each time I am greeted with ice

It is time to change my expectations and except the
revelation

I must release you for my freedom and my peace of
mind

No time for sorrows or regrets

I can't move forward looking back through my past
hanging on to empty dreams

It is impossible to rise up holding my head down

I am closing this chapter and moving forward

I release you!

What Really Matters

I have spent too much time trying to build a relationship with people

Desperately wanting to gain their acceptance that I never developed who I really am

Conforming and pretending so much that when I was asked the question "how do you see yourself?" The only response I had was "some days I don't even know."

I said it jokingly, but the sad thing is there was nothing but truth in that statement

The good thing is that it was a wakeup call for me

A call to the truth and honesty to myself

If you can't be true to you it is impossible to be true to anyone else

Overcomer

My past will not define me

My present will not confine me

But my faith in my future will set me free

This end is one step closer to my new beginning

This journey has been a trying time

It brought lots of pain and a mass of confusion but through it all I refuse to give up

Determined to make it through

Something in me believes this was not all in vain; that there is a lesson to be learned and an outcome worth fighting for

If nothing else my strength and survival, my dignity and power; my courage and self esteem

All of which each test tried to strip from me

I am stronger than I thought I was and able to endure more than I thought I could

I will live and not die

My experiences have provided me with knowledge I did not possess

Wisdom on how to apply what I have learned and an understanding that not every difficult situation was designed to destroy me but to refine me and identify what has been placed in me

As the refinery purifies gold, my trials pulled out the best in me

As my gifts and talents surface I will remember what has brought me here

Allowing my test to become my testimony

I am an overcomer.

Maturity

Maturity doesn't always come with age. It comes from experiencing life learning from your mistakes accepting when you are wrong and being willing to change those things that need changing.

Maturity comes from gaining an understanding and opening yourself up to correction. It comes when you take the blinders off and see things for what they are whether good, bad or indifferent.

Maturity comes when you can be true to yourself and others. When you can release your own selfishness and see the needs of others.

Maturity comes when you can make decisions with not only you in mind but all that are involved.

Maturity can recognize needs versus wants, love versus lust and allow wisdom to reveal and expose deception when it comes.

Age has only a small portion to do with maturity. The wiliness to truly grow up will allow someone to mature

The End..

Well here we are at the end, but this is where I begin my journey to a new life

Focusing on who I am and where I want to be

Operating outside of business as usual and exploring the world outside of the box

Denying fear any place to operate in my life

Embracing new views and perspectives

I am nervous and excited but looking forward to a new and better life

I believe every failure, disappointment, betrayal, lie, abandonment and deception has prepared me for this day

I will walk in success and victory; using every stumbling block as a steppingstone and a means to rise up and not stay down, improving every step of the way. The end of this journey is the start to a new beginning.

www.ingramcontent.com/pod-product-compliance
Lightning Source LLC
Chambersburg PA
CBHW060157070426
42447CB00033B/2182